RUDY RUETTIGER
THE WALK ON

RUDY RUETTIGER
THE WALK ON

Published in New York, New York, by Morgan James Publishing in association with Impact Publishing. Morgan James is a trademark of Morgan James, LLC. www.MorganJamesPublishing.com

The Morgan James Speakers Group can bring authors to your live event. For more information or to book an event visit The Morgan James Speakers Group at www.TheMorganJamesSpeakersGroup.com.

ISBN 9781642790931 paperback
ISBN 9781642790948 case laminate
ISBN 9781642790955 eBook
Library of Congress Control Number: 2018943779

In an effort to support local communities, raise awareness and funds, Morgan James Publishing donates a percentage of all book sales for the life of each book to Habitat for Humanity Peninsula and Greater Williamsburg.

Get involved today! Visit www.MorganJamesBuilds.com.

DNA FILMS PRESENTS

A REAL HEROES PRODUCTION

A FILM BY NICK NANTON

PUBLISHED BY MORGAN JAMES PUBLISHING

THIS IS A TRUE STORY

IN 1974 ONE KID FROM JOLIET, ILLINOIS
HAD A DREAM...

TO PLAY FOOTBALL FOR NOTRE DAME

TODAY, THE WORLD KNOWS HIM AS
RUDY.

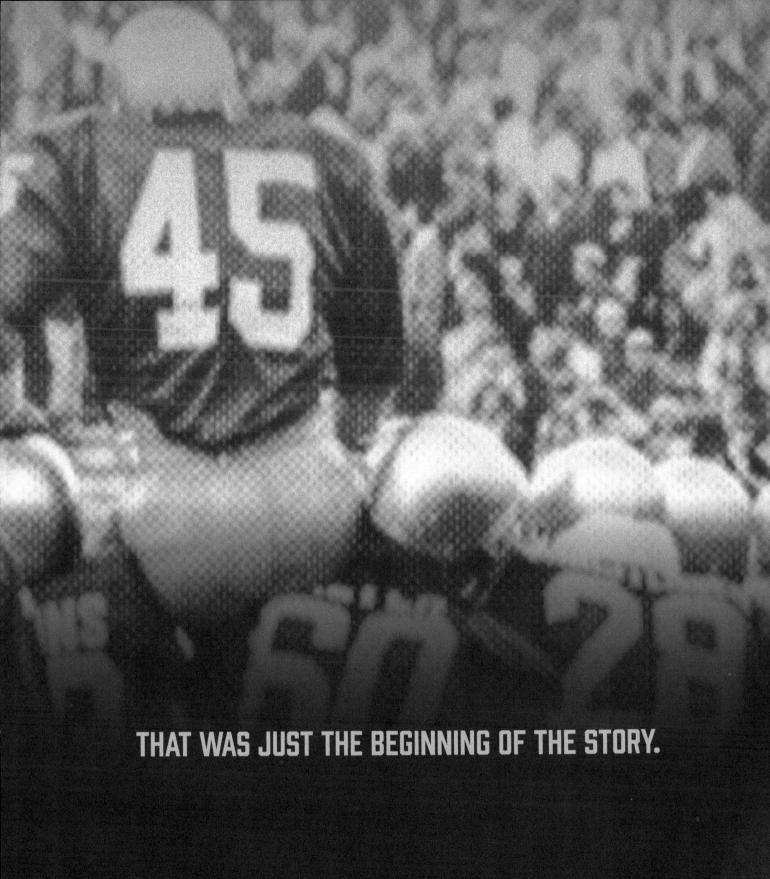

THAT WAS JUST THE BEGINNING OF THE STORY.

EXECUTIVE PRODUCERS JW DICKS NICK NANTON RANDY GARN

WRITTEN BY EMILY HACHE

EDITED BY NICK RUFF

DIRECTOR OF PHOTOGRAPHY   RAMY ROMANY

ADDITIONAL CINEMATOGRAPHERS
ROB HACHE   PARKER YATES
BRANDEN COLON   CARLO ALBERTO ORECCHIA
SHAWN VELA   ROGER STEELE   JEFF OTTUM

ASSOCIATE PRODUCERS   "JOHNNY B"   JOHN BRETTHAUER
RIZI TIMANE   TONY HANSMANN   CRAIG LACK

EXECUTIVE PRODUCERS   SOPHIA STAVRON   WILLIAM PARKER
GARY MARRIAGE JR.   PETE D'ARRUDA   RICHARD SEPPALA

EXECUTIVE PRODUCERS   ANDREW EILERS
EDWARD MAFOUD   MICHAEL JACZEWSKI

FIELD PRODUCER   KATIE TSCHOPP

RUBY ORIGINAL PAINTING BY DAVID SHINGLER

DIRECTED BY NICK NANTON

DAN "RUDY" RUETTIGER

"YOU KNOW EVERYONE LIVES A CERTAIN LIFE

and they're put in a certain culture. Once you're kind of locked in a culture, it's hard to think outside that culture. My dad, when Notre Dame was on, that's the only thing that was happening in that house. We went to church on Sunday, the priest gives a Notre Dame score. When your dad smiles you say to yourself, "Wow if I could do that, and make him smile, that'd be awesome," because my dad lived under stress. It was a very stressful life, but when he heard the Notre Dame score it gave him hope. So Notre Dame meant hope to me."

"WOW, IF I COULD DO THAT,
AND MAKE HIM SMILE, THAT'D
BE AWESOME."

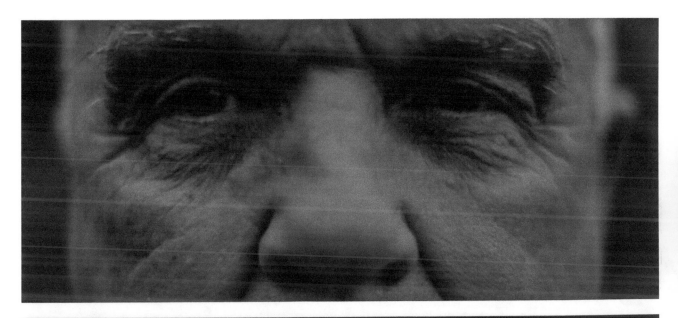

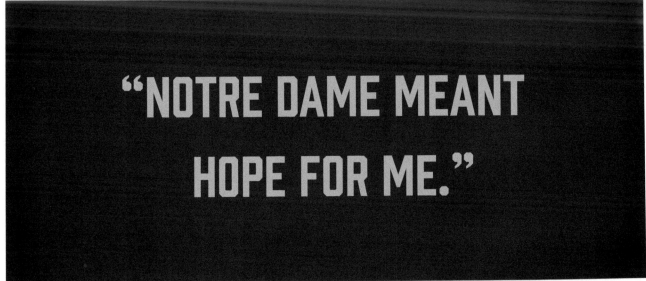

"NOTRE DAME MEANT HOPE FOR ME."

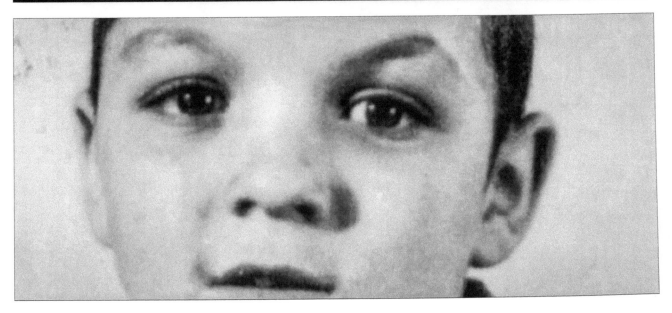

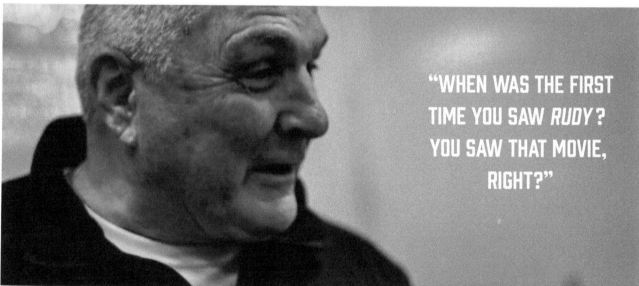

"WHEN WAS THE FIRST TIME YOU SAW *RUDY*? YOU SAW THAT MOVIE, RIGHT?"

CLASS YES

RUDY DID YOU LIKE IT?

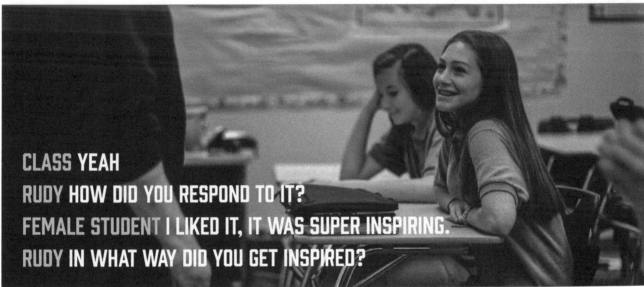

CLASS YEAH
RUDY HOW DID YOU RESPOND TO IT?
FEMALE STUDENT I LIKED IT, IT WAS SUPER INSPIRING.
RUDY IN WHAT WAY DID YOU GET INSPIRED?

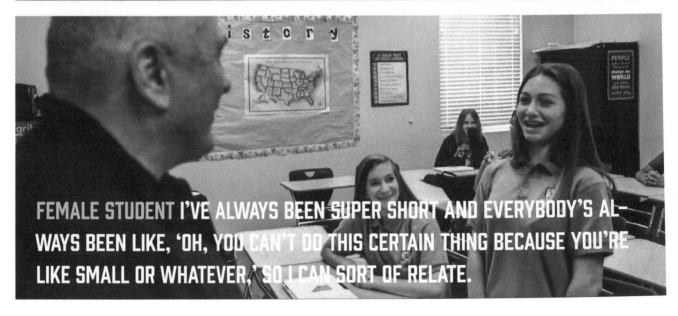

FEMALE STUDENT I'VE ALWAYS BEEN SUPER SHORT AND EVERYBODY'S ALWAYS BEEN LIKE, 'OH, YOU CAN'T DO THIS CERTAIN THING BECAUSE YOU'RE LIKE SMALL OR WHATEVER,' SO I CAN SORT OF RELATE.

RUDY Yeah. So you're still short? Really, can you stand up? Oh, you're the underdog girl, isn't that cool? What's the biggest message you got out of the movie *Rudy*? What would you say, or any of you guys...

FEMALE STUDENT Don't give up and don't let other people pressure you into not doing what you love to do.

RUDY That's so important, don't let them steal your joy. When I graduated from high school I wanted to go to Notre Dame. That was my dream. The problem was I was third in my class in high school, from the bottom. What are my chances of going to Notre Dame? None, because they accept, what? The top.

RUDY Yeah, and SATs they said the average SAT at Notre Dame was 1440. I didn't take them because the teacher said I was too stupid. I believed it until one day someone looked at the little things I did. The little things: how I made my bed, how I folded my socks, how I shined my shoes. I was in the Navy, and a drill instructor came up to me and said you're a good guy, you're a leader of all these shipmates. He gave me

confidence and then I started dreaming again. When you give someone confidence...you're key to dreaming is confidence. Remember that, confidence. People don't care how smart you are, they want to know how much you care, remember that. How much you care! And, when you do that you're gonna succeed, because people are gonna help you succeed and people come around you and help you get to places you never thought you could go. I got to Notre Dame because I found another way. It's like going off to Hollywood saying, "I'm gonna make a movie." People laughed, but it wasn't about me, it was about you, it's about your struggles. It's about how I could help you get through your struggles. It's about self-esteem, it's about believing in yourself, it's about not quitting, it's about leaping out on faith and going for your dream. Don't ask permission for your dream, just go get it, does that help?

"DON'T ASK FOR PERMISSION FOR YOUR DREAM, JUST GO GET IT!"

"I GOT TO NOTRE DAME BECAUSE I FOUND ANOTHER WAY."

TERRY GANNON
SPORTS BROADCASTER

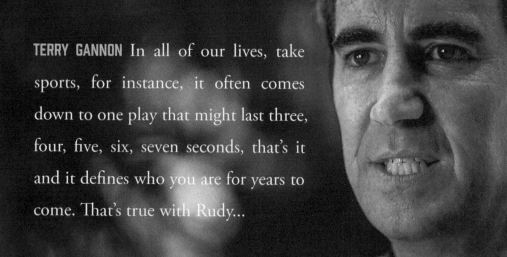

TERRY GANNON In all of our lives, take sports, for instance, it often comes down to one play that might last three, four, five, six, seven seconds, that's it and it defines who you are for years to come. That's true with Rudy...

HOWEVER, TO GET TO THOSE SEVEN SECONDS IT TOOK A LIFETIME OF DREAMING AND BELIEVING WHEN NO ONE ELSE DID.

SOUTH BEND, INDIANA

RUDY This is a magical path, we call it the magical roadway to Holy Cross because you felt at peace right here. You didn't feel intimidated, you didn't feel like anyone was trying to stop you, you're just still feeling good and powerful that you could be at Notre Dame someday. There's a reason for that, I think here you're... there's no interference of anybody telling you what you can do, what you can't do, but it's just a good feeling. And you would walk this path with no worries until you got to the end of this path then, reality happened. You got to go to school, you got to do good, you gotta get the grades. So the anxiety would start up again, then it stopped once you start putting foot on that campus again, Notre Dame, it felt good and powerful. We had no worries, all we have to do is do the work and be consistent and be patient, ask for help and we can get it done. You wouldn't be here if you didn't have the talent or ability, you just need the consistency and the belief in yourself. This is where it came from, right here.

Up here we're at the stations of the cross. Calvary, we call it Calvary, you'll see it right up here. The impossible did become pos-

sible at this point. A lot of people never understood what I was doing, thought it was such a wild dream, wild road. My dad would always say, "Ah that's for rich kids, great athletes, it's not for the Ruettigers," but I wanted to show him it is for the Ruettigers. It's for anybody who had a dream that was willing to work hard, and that is why this works. You can give that back to other people, positive encouragement. You see students and you kind of say, "Thank you for the smile," that smile of encouragement. It kind of helped you along the way, when things were tough or when things weren't going your way, but isn't life that way? Life is about not everything's gonna go your way. So, that's my journey. It starts right here and ends up at Notre Dame.

"IT'S NOT WHERE YOU START,

IT'S WHERE YOU END UP."

DICK VITALE
ESPN COLLEGE BASKETBALL ANALYST

DICK VITALE I don't care who you talk about. I don't care who you talk about whether he's famous, whether he's rich, they've all had some ups and downs. We don't know many of the problems they have. They may have lost someone they loved. They might have had a job initially that they hated. They might not have enjoyed the people they worked with. They might have friendships that went south on them. They might have had a divorce case in their family. Everybody's got hits, but how you bounce back from that adversity is the difference between a champ, many times, and a chump. And Rudy's story gives you that kind of inspiration. Here's a guy that would not take no. Rudy never ever allowed people to tell him you can't make it at Notre Dame, you can't go to that school, you're not going to get there, you're not going to make it. He didn't allow that to bring him down. So many people allow others to dictate their future. It didn't happen with Rudy.

SO MANY PEOPLE ALLOW OTHERS TO DICTATE THEIR FUTURE.

IT DIDN'T HAPPEN WITH RUDY. –DICK VITALE

DENNIS "D-BOB" MCGOWAN
RUDY'S BEST FRIEND

DENNIS "D-BOB" MCGOWAN Rudy, to me, is just a great friend. But to the world, the name Rudy has almost become an adjective. When you watch ESPN or Sports Illustrated you'll hear a reference to a kid who doesn't play much, that plays hard, he's a Rudy. I keep thinking one of these days it's going to be in Webster's Dictionary. Everybody relates to that name.

RICHIE CONTARTESI
OLE MISS WALK ON ('08–'10)

RICHIE CONTARTESI When you're on the one-yard line. When you have nothing left in your tank. When you've given up on yourself. When everybody else has given up on you...

WHEN YOU'VE HIT ROCK BOTTOM, IT'S THE ONES THAT TAKE ONE MORE STEP THAT GET THE GOLD. THAT GET THE DREAM.

LARRY MORIARTY
ND RUNNING BACK ('80-'82)

LARRY MORIARTY Anybody that's been around Rudy all you have to do is look at his eyes. He may look like he's soft and gentle, but he's determined. He's always been determined. There's no stopping Rudy, he never quits, and I had the same makeup. I didn't quit and I wanted to be somebody, and...

I WANTED TO BE LIKE RUDY. NOT THE MOVIE RUDY, THE REAL RUDY.

RUDY Well, when you have six brothers and seven sisters, you know, you got to learn to position yourself: to get the first meal, to get the first pair of underwear coming out of the washer. You know, you fight for the little things. Now here's my point, coming from a large family, I'm the oldest boy. In the movie, we showed it a little different. You're set back quite a bit as an older child because parents are very protective. My parents were very structured, very disciplined. But fortunately, my mother, early on, gave us dreams. And she said "Dream big," but unfortunately my dad thought differently. He thought you get a good job, and you be an honorable guy and you'll be fine. I just didn't want a job, I wanted something much different. Maybe playing for the Yankees... but that wasn't possible. But, Notre Dame, maybe Notre Dame... and that's not possible. So, I kind of lost sight of [those dreams]. So people who have big dreams can connect to the fact that if you define yourself, redefine yourself and learn more about believing in yourself, those dreams do come back.

THE RUETTIGER BROTHERS

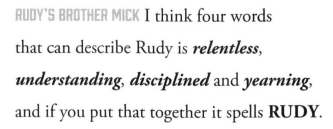

RUDY'S BROTHER MICK I think four words that can describe Rudy is *relentless*, *understanding*, *disciplined* and *yearning*, and if you put that together it spells **RUDY**.

RUDY'S BROTHER FRANCIS We used to go watch him play at Joliet Catholic football, and he was a pretty good football player in high school. I always admired that because he was always the smallest guy out there, but he was one of the toughest guys. So I'd try to emulate myself after him in everything he did, whether it was right or wrong, I tried to emulate it.

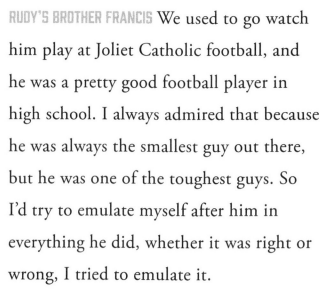

R
RELENTLESS

U
UNDERSTANDING

D
DISCIPLINED

Y
YEARNING

RUDY Being part of a big family you got a lot of criticism, that's what it was like, you got criticized a lot because of your behavior in school. The teacher would say in front of my parents, "Your kid's unteachable," because I didn't score well in the entrance tests, "but we'll give him a try." And I heard that. I said, "Wow, I must be stupid. I'm not stupid, because I can think things out, I mean why are they saying I'm slow? I'm just as smart as that guy, but different maybe, but I'm okay."

Well dyslexia is a learning disorder and you have to know how to teach that, but all your great ones, all the big guys, all your visionaries have dyslexia. Because dyslexia means you don't pay attention to the small stuff. Once I learned that I got excited, I'm awesome, because I had a vision. I could see myself way before it happens. I could see me doing things way before it happened. But it's hard to step back and say, "But you got to do the homework, you got to do the little things, Rudy."

RUDY'S BROTHER, TIM Mom and Dad's work ethic was exceptional. We never wanted for anything. They gave us all jobs to do, and if we didn't fulfill those jobs there was hell to pay at the end of the day.

RUDY It was stressful. Working three jobs, had to put food on the table, clothes on our back. You know what was great about my father, he also coached little league doing all that. My mother was the president of the women's club. So they were all so involved with us.

RUDY'S BROTHER, FRANCIS We had a huge side lot that we made into a baseball field. Both my parents were pretty athletic and they used to play hardball baseball right with us.

RUDY'S BROTHER, MICK Growing up in Joliet, you're going to play football. You know that's what everybody aspired to be was a football player or a baseball player.

RUDY'S BROTHER, JOHN Blue-collar steel.

RUDY'S BROTHER, MICK Blue collar, yeah, and if you didn't play football, you know it was just... it was just the times... you weren't looked upon as a tough guy.

TERRY GANNON Joliet was the ultimate blue-collar, steel mill town and you had the prison, Stateville Prison. We were known for two things. They were the people who made up the fabric of this country, still are. I grew up with the Ruettiger family, in Joliet, Illinois. My dad coached and taught at Joliet Catholic, coached Rudy, taught him as well. So I've known Rudy and his brothers since I was yea high. I mean that's a crew. You think about that family, and how big that family is, you know all of those brothers... and when they get together the one thing that comes through, they bust each other's chops all the time, yes, but there's pride.

FRANCIS I'd be daydreaming out the window counting the train cars go by. You know, we had a train track by the high school we went to, and I didn't pay attention what the teacher said. I didn't care at the time, you know what I mean? I just wanted to make it through, because he was my idol and that's how he made it through. You get, you know what I'm saying?

TERRY GANNON When you go to his brother Francis' gym he's got up on the wall article after article, picture after picture, about what Danny did at Notre Dame.

FRANCIS There are some great memories in here. This is my office in here. Actually, I had a little, not a shrine, but an area dedicated to his college career at Notre Dame. An article about him, that's him running down the field there. These are all dedicated to him, the movie's up there.

MICK When I was growing up I was seven years younger than him so all you did was see him play football, water ski and play baseball. I think he was an outstanding athlete. I think he was the best athlete out of all the brothers, me being number seven and him being number one, but when you saw him play you got to believe, you can't even contest that, don't contest that.

RUDY In high school I was just a common player, but I did make all-conference. Small guy, I played guard. We went ten and zero my senior year, so we had a decent football team. We had a lot of confidence, but

I WAS NOT A STAR, I WAS NOT A CANDIDATE FOR ANY COLLEGE.

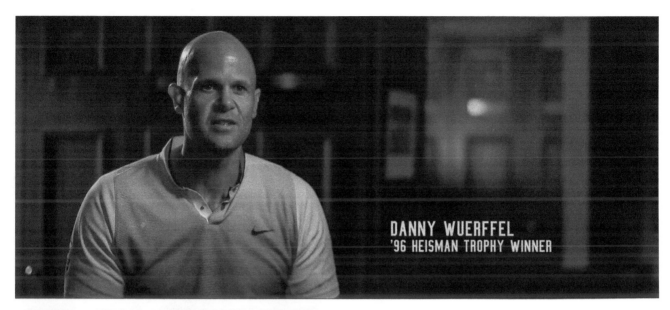

DANNY WUERFFEL Well I think when you're young you just have these ideas, these dreams, that life is just sort of going to work out for you, especially if you apply yourself to something. And I think you know life slowly begins, it can, to beat you down. It's very difficult. I'll never forget my dad saying these three words over and over, "You know, Danny, life is tough." I hated when he said that, and I still hate it, but I think that's part of the reality that you have to internalize and learn and the things that you think are important or the things that matter to you usually don't come easy.

RUDY Okay after I graduated from high school I didn't have a choice, can't go to college, so plan B go to work. I went to work, got a good job. Power plant, security, brotherhood of electrical workers - you have a job no matter what. I had security. Well 1969: The war, Vietnam. My buddies were going over there and not coming home. Kind of upset me. I said I'm not going to get drafted, I'm going to join. So I went down to the Navy recruiter. Unbeknownst to my mom and dad, went down there, the guy was awesome, the Navy recruiter said, "Dude, if you can fold underwear, shine shoes, make a bed, you can be in the Navy." I said, "I can do all that, sir." He said, "Well you're in the Navy."

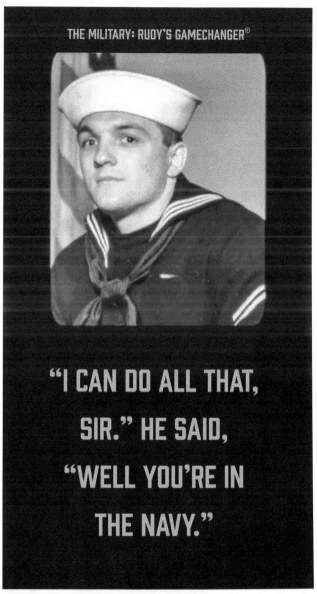

THE MILITARY: RUDY'S GAMECHANGER®

"I CAN DO ALL THAT, SIR." HE SAID, "WELL YOU'RE IN THE NAVY."

NEWS ANNOUNCER THE PRESIDENT HAS ASKED THAT THE DESTROYER
FORCE BE DOUBLED AND HE'S ISSUED INSTRUCTIONS THAT IN THE EVENT
OF A FURTHER ATTACK UPON OUR VESSELS IN INTERNATIONAL WATERS WE
ARE TO RESPOND WITH THE OBJECTIVE OF DESTROYING THE ATTACKERS.

RUDY'S BROTHER, TIM All I know is, at that time, I was very nervous. It was scary because we had a lot of friends that were going, and Rudy joined the Navy. It was, you know, it's nervous because you don't know what's going to happen, and I always thought that would be the worst place to be is on a ship, because you have nowhere to go, you know, if something hits it. It was a nervous time, but my dad was a World War II herd gunner, so he sort of was able to put your mind at ease, you know, about that stuff.

I SAID, "SIR DID YOU GO TO NOTRE DAME."

HE SAID, "YES I DID."

"IS THAT YOUR RING?"

"YES."

I SAID, "HOW DO I GET ONE OF THOSE?"

HE SAYS, "STUDY HARD BOY, STUDY HARD."

"BUT, SIR, I DIDN'T DO VERY GOOD IN SCHOOL."

"DOESN'T MATTER, IF YOU WANT TO GO THERE YOU'LL FIND A WAY."

RUDY Thank God I went to the Navy, man, got to see the world on a destroyer. They didn't tell me I would get seasick, but I did. I'm in the Navy now, I see this Lieutenant Commander with a Notre Dame ring. Now, here's where he could have ruined my dream easily, when I asked this question:

RUDY MEET AND GREET DINNER
NOTRE DAME

GUEST WHY DID YOU PERSIST WHEN OTHER PEOPLE WOULD QUIT? HOW DID YOU KEEP YOURSELF GOING?

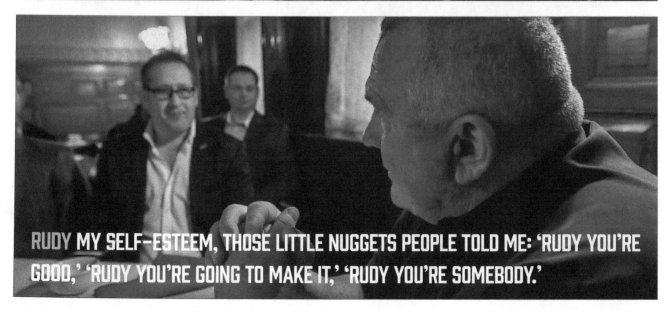

RUDY MY SELF-ESTEEM, THOSE LITTLE NUGGETS PEOPLE TOLD ME: 'RUDY YOU'RE GOOD,' 'RUDY YOU'RE GOING TO MAKE IT,' 'RUDY YOU'RE SOMEBODY.'

RUDY I kind of lost that feeling, when my teacher kind of pointed me out in front of all my friends because I didn't do my homework, and she wanted to know who the fifth president was (that's what we were supposed to go home and study).

I was home run champion, I was Mickey Mantle, man. You don't care. I beat all my neighbors man, I'm the guy. "Who's the fifth president, Rudy?" I didn't know and I didn't care.

GUEST And today it's over.

RUDY Yeah, yeah so she made me stand up and sit in the back of the room, that's the day I quit dreaming. I went through all of high school, graduated third in my class from the bottom. You can't go to Notre Dame when you're third from the bottom, you didn't take the SAT, you don't have a class rank, you don't have any money, and you're not that great of an athlete. But, what happens, you're the leader of all these ship mates? What does that do? It gave me confidence. I started dreaming again.

RUDY'S BROTHER, FRANCIS You know, he kind of put his dream aside for a while, when he went to the service; everything was collapsing around him. So, he got his dream back, I think, when he was in the service, and then when he came back he had to go back to work.

RUDY Working in a power plant meant security, but that's not what I wanted. Swing shifts, days, middle of the day you gotta go, night shift, I didn't like it. And then you hang around the "why" guys that say, "See, I told you, Rudy, that's a stupid dream," "I told you you're stupid," "You're crazy"... you know, all those things, and you get into arguments with your guys at work. One day the accident happens, and that's where I learned life is too short. Very calm day, not windy, very nice day. We get a phone call from the control room, "One tower, go out and fix it." So, wow, and I told Sisco, "Can you take the equipment out mechanically, I'll take it out electrically." He went out there, before me, to the coal yard and saw the problem. He said, "Yeah, I can fix that."

Well, what he doesn't realize, when those boilers call for fuel, they want their fuel.

Because what it does, the conveyor vibrates, shakes coal on the conveyor, sends it up to a crusher, crushes the coal, then pours it into ovens and they burn it up, melt it, and steam comes out. He stepped on that conveyor when the system called for fuel. Don't go anywhere near there when that system calls for fuel, because everything starts up. He stepped on and saw the problem and said, "I can fix that," to save me from having to come out there. He took a shortcut, and the system called for fuel, it dragged him into eight feeders, broke his neck. I just happened to be walking out when I saw his body, right before it got to the crusher. I tripped the conveyor, tried to revive him, and that's the day I changed my whole life.

"DON'T LIVE IN REGRET,"

that's what the guy kept saying to me, that died, "don't live in regret." That stuck with me. We live in regret, most of us. You go to the graveyards in America, a lot of dreams are buried.

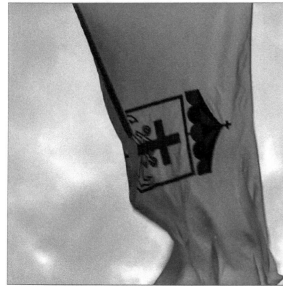

RUDY'S BROTHER, FRANCIS He just kept his dream alive, and then after Sisco had died, which he was involved with as far as trying to revive him on the conveyor belt, it was like a couple days later he told my dad that he's quitting his job and he's going, you know,

"I'M GOING TO NOTRE DAME AND PLAY FOOTBALL."

CUT TO: RUDY WALKING NOTRE DAME CAMPUS

RUDY HEY GUYS, MORNING. CUBS, ARE YOU A CUBS FAN?

GIRL ON CAMPUS YEAH

RUDY I LOVE IT. WHERE ARE YOU FROM, CHICAGO?

GIRL ON CAMPUS CHICAGO.

RUDY WHAT'S YOUR FAVORITE SPORTS MOVIE?

GIRL ON CAMPUS *RUDY!*

RUDY ALL RIGHT, ALL RIGHT!

RUDY MORNING GIRLS. GOOD LUCK ON YOUR FINALS. YEAH, FINALS ARE COMING UP, RIGHT?
GIRL ON CAMPUS YEP!

RUDY SMILE, MY BROTHER. YOU'RE AT NOTRE DAME.

"I WANNA SHOW
YOU SOMETHING
REALLY COOL, GUYS.
SO FOLLOW ME."

RUDY THAT LITTLE BUILDING RIGHT ACROSS THE STREET, SEE THAT BUILDING RIGHT THERE?

RUDY THAT'S WHERE I SAW NOTRE DAME FOR THE FIRST TIME.

RUDY WE CAME HERE ON A HIGH SCHOOL RETREAT. LOOK RIGHT TO THE LEFT, WHAT DO YOU SEE?

RUDY A POWER PLANT. AT 10 DEGREES, THAT'S WHERE I CAME FROM, THE POWER PLANT.

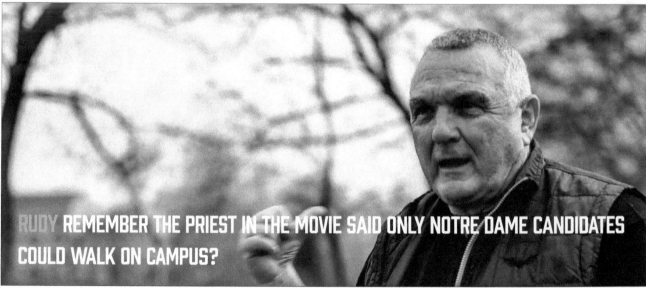

RUDY REMEMBER THE PRIEST IN THE MOVIE SAID ONLY NOTRE DAME CANDIDATES COULD WALK ON CAMPUS?

RUDY I SNUCK ON CAMPUS.

RUDY

"HERE'S WHAT'S AWESOME ABOUT FINDING ANOTHER WAY. YOU DON'T KNOW THAT OTHER WAY. BUT WHEN YOU'RE POSITIVE AND YOU POSITION YOURSELF, NOW, TO WIN, THE ANSWER'S RIGHT IN FRONT OF YOU."

RUDY'S BROTHER, MICK I don't think Dad wanted him to go, because he's leaving a good job. He didn't understand the chance Rudy wanted to take in his own life. My dad wanted every kid that he brought up to be secure, have a family, and live a good life and contribute back to society.

RUDY'S BROTHER, FRANCIS You know, back then everybody used to think he was crazy. Because he was so small, he didn't have the grades, you know what I mean?

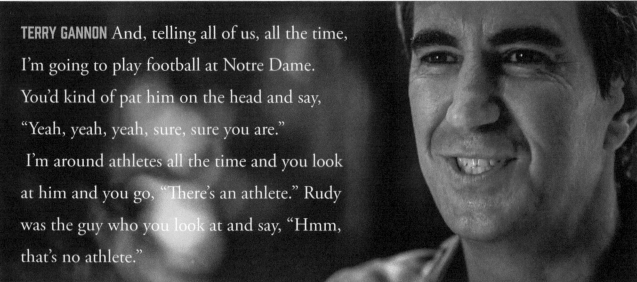

TERRY GANNON And, telling all of us, all the time, I'm going to play football at Notre Dame. You'd kind of pat him on the head and say, "Yeah, yeah, yeah, sure, sure you are." I'm around athletes all the time and you look at him and you go, "There's an athlete." Rudy was the guy who you look at and say, "Hmm, that's no athlete."

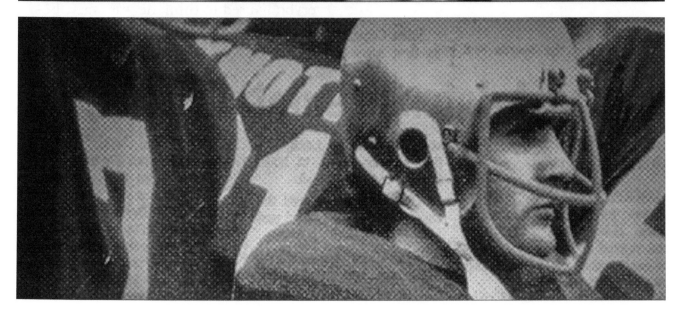

RUDY RUETTIGER: THE WALK ON

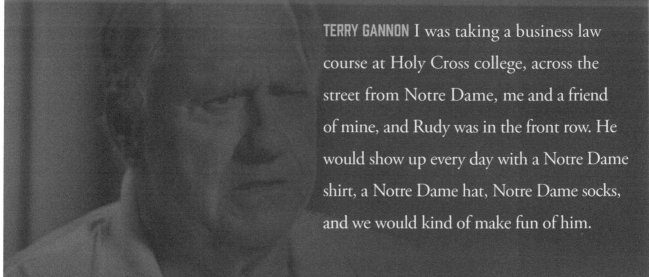

TERRY GANNON I was taking a business law course at Holy Cross college, across the street from Notre Dame, me and a friend of mine, and Rudy was in the front row. He would show up every day with a Notre Dame shirt, a Notre Dame hat, Notre Dame socks, and we would kind of make fun of him.

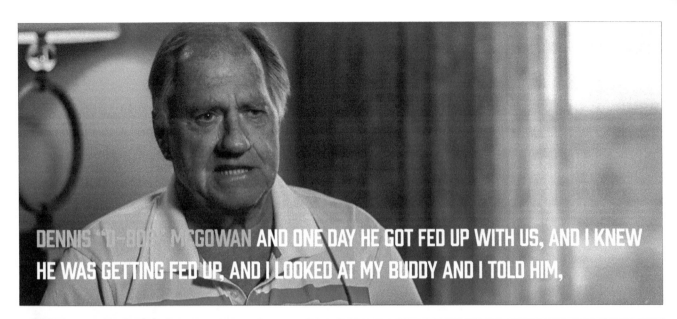

DENNIS "D-BOB" MCGOWAN AND ONE DAY HE GOT FED UP WITH US, AND I KNEW HE WAS GETTING FED UP, AND I LOOKED AT MY BUDDY AND I TOLD HIM,

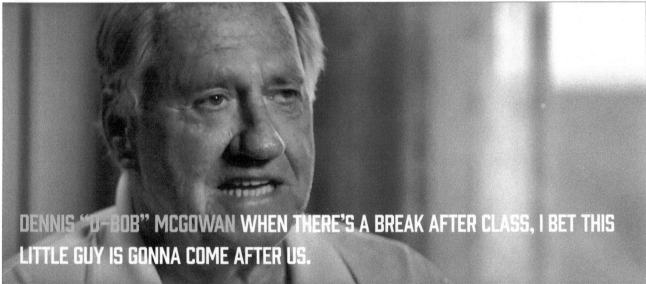

DENNIS "D-BOB" MCGOWAN WHEN THERE'S A BREAK AFTER CLASS, I BET THIS LITTLE GUY IS GONNA COME AFTER US.

DENNIS "D-BOB" MCGOWAN SO WE'RE OUTSIDE THE CLASSROOM DURING A BREAK, AND SURE ENOUGH, HERE HE COMES AFTER US.

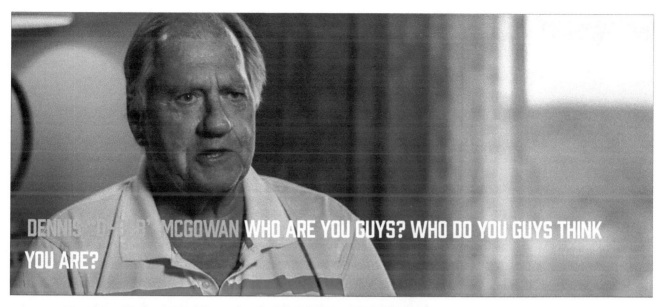

DENNIS "DeBoy" McGOWAN WHO ARE YOU GUYS? WHO DO YOU GUYS THINK YOU ARE?

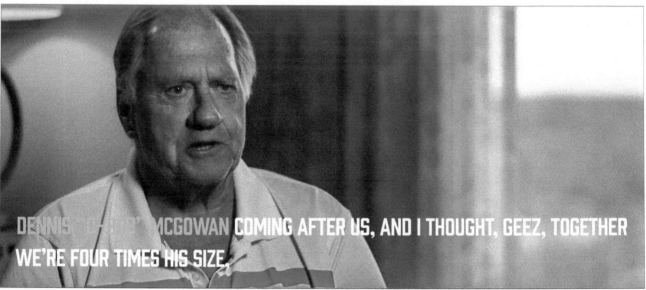

DENNIS "DeBoy" McGOWAN COMING AFTER US, AND I THOUGHT, GEEZ, TOGETHER WE'RE FOUR TIMES HIS SIZE,

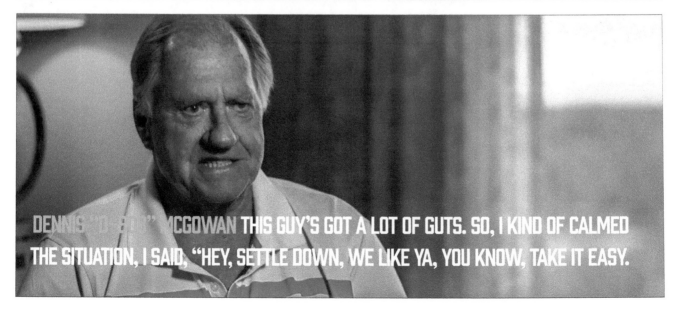

DENNIS "DeBoy" McGOWAN THIS GUY'S GOT A LOT OF GUTS. SO, I KIND OF CALMED THE SITUATION, I SAID, "HEY, SETTLE DOWN, WE LIKE YA, YOU KNOW, TAKE IT EASY.

RUDY AND D-BOB REUNION PARTY
ORLANDO

CUT TO: REUNION PARTY

RUDY We met 40 something years ago at Notre Dame.

DENNIS "D-BOB" MCGOWAN At Holy Cross Junior College. He was trying to get in Notre Dame and I was taking a law class. And I had to get him through...

RUDY He didn't, no, no, no.

DENNIS "D-BOB" MCGOWAN He comes from a family of 14, so there was no support at home. So, he had to hustle his way through school.

RUDY Well, you connect with guys like D-Bob because he understood where you were coming from. The elite, and I call the entitled, wouldn't understand this. So he had to hang around with guys who understood.

DENNIS "D-BOB" MCGOWAN That's why you could never beat him in a fight. He had seven brothers... well there were seven brothers.

RUDY Six.

DENNIS "D-BOB" MCGOWAN He had six brothers, there were seven boys.

RUDY And seven sisters.

DENNIS "D-BOB" MCGOWAN And they had a big dorm room, and all the boys slept in one room. So every morning there were three or four fist fights, usually, before you got out of the bedroom. So, I've tried to beat him up three or four times and without success. He rolls up like an armadillo. And you'd beat on him for about an hour, and then he uncoils and lets you have it. And by the way, I had a lot of respect for him.

So the next day, the football team was practicing in the stadium, they very seldom do that, and they don't let anybody in. I look up and there's Rudy sitting on the top rung in the stadium by himself. I walk all the way up there. He doesn't look at me. He doesn't say anything. I sit down next to him, I say, "Hey, Rudy, what's wrong?" He says, "Dennis, one day I'm going to play down there." And somehow I believed it.

🎬 CUT TO: VARIOUS SHOTS OF NOTRE DAME

RUDY Now, you have to go back to your mind-set and say, "Well, I don't know, junior college, that's not for a smart kid, that's for dumb kids, because that's what they would say in high school. Oh, dummies go to junior college." Well, because I'm in the Navy, because of what I learned, I quit listening to that goofy thinking. Brother John was the President of Holy Cross Junior College. Brother John was a good Brother. He saw the spirit in me. He said, "Rudy, can you commit four semesters here?"

I said, "yes."

Then he told me the criteria, what I had to do. You have to do some work. A lot of work, because people who want to go across the street work hard.

I said, "Brother, I gotta get to Notre Dame now. I gotta try out for the football team." He said, "Rudy, Rudy, Rudy, first things first, you need to get your grades up, then I'll endorse you going to Notre Dame."

I said, "I know, Brother, but I'll be too old."

"You're never too old, Rudy, you're never too old. If this is what you want, you keep that

attitude up, we can do this."

I believed him. And we did it.

RUDY My first four tests at Holy Cross, I failed. "Uh Oh, uh oh," I said. This is not good. So I went in to see Brother John.

I said, "Brother, it's not working."

He said, "Well, what's not working?"

"I failed my first four tests."

He said, "Ah, don't worry about it. Start developing a relationship with your Professors."

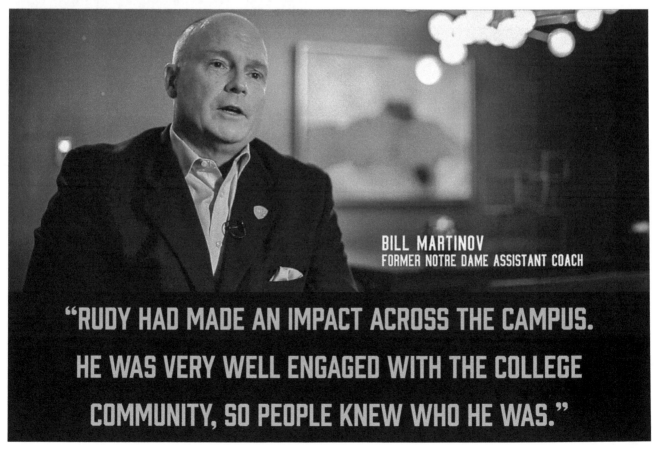

BILL MARTINOV
FORMER NOTRE DAME ASSISTANT COACH

"RUDY HAD MADE AN IMPACT ACROSS THE CAMPUS. HE WAS VERY WELL ENGAGED WITH THE COLLEGE COMMUNITY, SO PEOPLE KNEW WHO HE WAS."

TERRY GANNON I think Rudy really spent more time on Notre Dame campus than Holy Cross campus.

RUDY'S BROTHER, FRANCIS I used to walk around with him on campus and they actually thought he was part of the program, over there. He made himself feel right at home.

BILL MARTINOV And then because they knew who he was, they knew his dream and his story.

TERRY GANNON There's no way that you would think that this guy doesn't go to Notre Dame.

VOICE OVER He boxed one year without being a student.

VOICE OVER He was not just football, but he was in the Bengal Bouts.

RUDY Well, the Bengal Bouts, I fought for two years. And my senior year I won it. But, my sophomore year, over at Holy Cross, I snuck in.

They said, "Rudy, where do you go to school?"

I said, "I don't go here yet."

They said, "You can't box, sorry."

I'm telling you [boxing] builds your self-esteem. I was against a couple of football players and beat 'em. And that's where I got the respect of the football players.

MIKE BONIFER
FORMER CLASSMATE

MIKE BONIFER Here comes a guy that was probably seven or eight years older than most of the students, who had learned to fight brawling in the Navy. So the bell would ring and Rudy would sprint across the ring, and people would crumble under the onslaught. They didn't even have time to get their fists up, because

RUDY WAS LIKE POPEYE-ING THE SHIT OUT OF THEM.

That's when the Rudy chant started; because people would so look forward to this guy from out of nowhere who is sprinting across the ring and Navy brawling his way through the Bengal Bouts.

RUDY'S BROTHER, FRANCIS I'd go down there on the weekends and visit him. And he says, "I'm playing football." I'm thinking, he's playing football at Notre Dame. He said, "I've got practice." So I go out to practice, I was watching them practice, I see all these, about 20 to 30 kids running out there with these gold helmets, but they're all nicked up and stuff. I was thinking, this don't look like Notre Dame football to me. Here it was inner hall Football. The kids made it up, you know they play in their helmets, get all excited you know. I said,

"YOU AIN'T PLAYING FOOTBALL, YOU'RE INNER HALL FOOTBALL." I SAID, "WHAT'S THIS ALL ABOUT?"

HE SAID, "WELL, I HAVEN'T MADE IT TO SCHOOL YET."

NOTRE

DAME

"WHEN YOU START VISUALIZING WHAT
YOU WANT IN LIFE, I'M TELLING YOU,
IT'S GOING TO WORK." –RUDY

DR. LUTHER SNAVELY
DIRECTOR OF ND BANDS ('87–'01)

DR. LUTHER SNAVELY It's the little things. It's the little things that make a big difference. The thing about the Rudy story, that's really important, is that a person who works hard and dreams and tries his very best has a chance to be rewarded. That he doesn't have to give up because he can't run the fastest, or he's not the strongest, or he can't jump the highest, but that he just keeps working and trying, and working and trying. Good things might happen to him.

TERRY GANNON He knew he was going to get it done. One way or another he was going to get it done.

DENNIS "D-BOB" MCGOWAN The other fallacy in the movie, if there's such a thing as a fallacy, is that we only portrayed three times

of him getting rejected. He was rejected more than 50 times.

RUDY After getting two rejection letters, you're still doubting a little bit, is this really going to happen? The belief level starts sinking a little bit. Really, you think Brother will recommend me? You think that's the real deal? I'm working hard for this.

And because of that attitude, I start building relationships again, with the Dean here, at Notre Dame. That kind of looked at your transcripts and looked at the people who make the decisions. I built relationships with the secretaries. I made sure they knew who I was. In fact, the Dean saw me every day at the office and said,

"What are you doing here every day?"

I said, "Just so you know me."

He said, "I don't want to see you every day."

I said, "I know it. The day you don't see me is the day I get in."

RUDY NOW WE'RE GOING TO WALK AROUND HERE AND YOU CAN SEE THE GOLDEN DOME HERE.

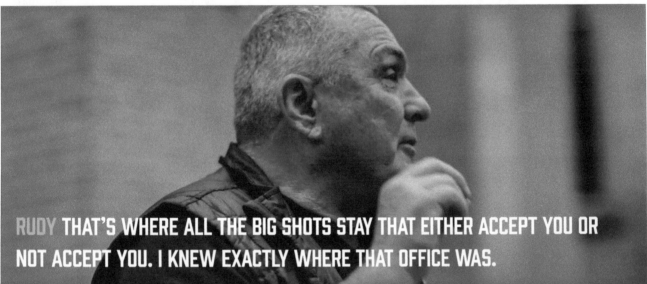

RUDY THAT'S WHERE ALL THE BIG SHOTS STAY THAT EITHER ACCEPT YOU OR NOT ACCEPT YOU. I KNEW EXACTLY WHERE THAT OFFICE WAS.

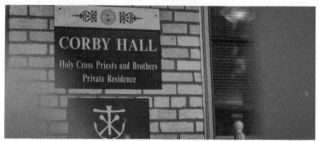

RUDY'S BROTHER, MICK I remember the first night that he got his rejection letter and we had a 1966 Buick station wagon with a bat that propped up the front seat. He took that '66 wagon and headed down to Notre Dame. It was probably about 9:30-10:00, I believe, at night, he was so upset that he got that letter.

🎬 **RUDY REENACTING THE NIGHT HE FIRST GOT HIS REJECTION LETTER**

RUDY 11:00, coach, this is a big move here. I'm knocking on that door there waking up the Priest. You need a lot of courage to do that. Watch this. So you walk up here. I'm beside myself. I've got to know, right? So all I do. I look and I knock and I knock. Finally, a Priest opens the door.

🎬 **WOMAN UNEXPECTEDLY OPENS DOOR**

RUDY [TALKING TO WOMAN] How about that? Is that awesome? I'm just showing them where I came and knocked on the door at 11:00 at night, I'm Rudy.

WOMAN You are Rudy, oh my gosh, I might start crying.

83

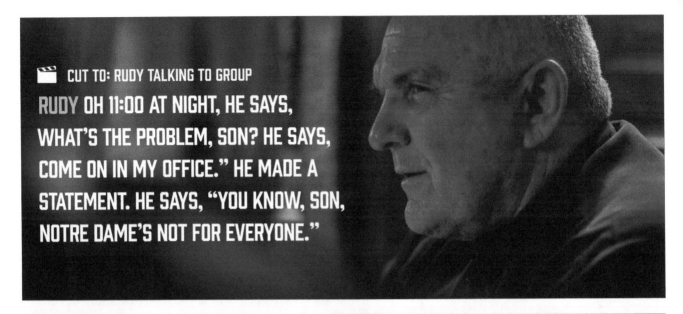

CUT TO: RUDY TALKING TO GROUP

RUDY OH 11:00 AT NIGHT, HE SAYS, WHAT'S THE PROBLEM, SON? HE SAYS, COME ON IN MY OFFICE." HE MADE A STATEMENT. HE SAYS, "YOU KNOW, SON, NOTRE DAME'S NOT FOR EVERYONE."

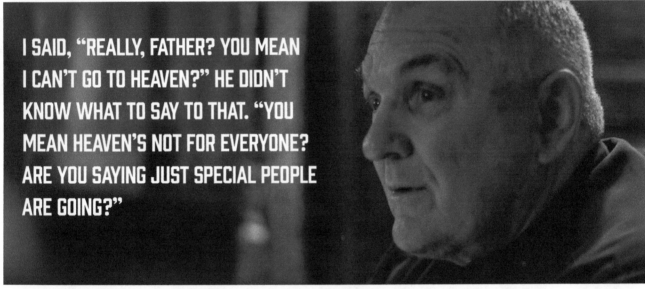

I SAID, "REALLY, FATHER? YOU MEAN I CAN'T GO TO HEAVEN?" HE DIDN'T KNOW WHAT TO SAY TO THAT. "YOU MEAN HEAVEN'S NOT FOR EVERYONE? ARE YOU SAYING JUST SPECIAL PEOPLE ARE GOING?"

HE SAID, "THAT'S NOT TRUE."

"I'LL TELL YA WHAT, LET'S CALL YOUR PARENTS AND LET THEM KNOW WHERE YOU ARE. DO YOUR PARENTS KNOW YOU'RE..."

I SAID, "NO."

HE SAID, "LET'S CALL, LET 'EM KNOW."

RUDY I DECIDED NOT TO GO HOME. I STAYED UP ALL NIGHT AT THE GROTTO, PRAYING. STARTED LIGHTING THOSE CANDLES, PRAYING ALL NIGHT.

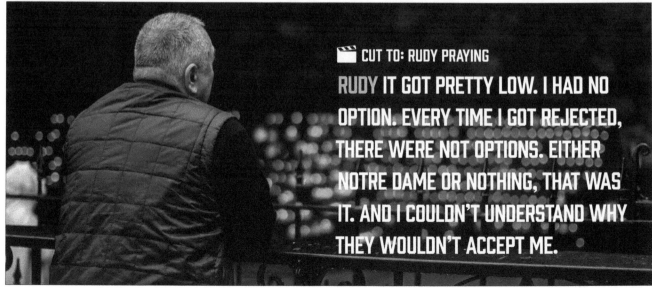

🎬 CUT TO: RUDY PRAYING

RUDY IT GOT PRETTY LOW. I HAD NO OPTION. EVERY TIME I GOT REJECTED, THERE WERE NOT OPTIONS. EITHER NOTRE DAME OR NOTHING, THAT WAS IT. AND I COULDN'T UNDERSTAND WHY THEY WOULDN'T ACCEPT ME.

RUDY I asked the Brother, "Why are they doing this?"

He said, "I told you four semesters, Rudy." And he said, "There's no negotiation on that."

And I walked from the grotto over to the athletic convocation center, I'm sitting there waiting for Ara so I can tell him, I'm going to play football for you. I was determined now, after he said Notre Dame's not for everyone, right?

Okay, there's the football office, it used to be right there, see that? That's where Ara, that last window was his office. When I walked up to his office, I saw his car pull up. I said, "I can't do it." He came walking up, I went right behind those bushes. I didn't want him to see me. "No, I can't do it." I said, "No, you are going to do it." Because of that, as he walked in, as that gentleman's walking in, I followed right behind him. And he opened that door, I caught that door right before it slammed. And I went in.

So I walked in there, he's sitting behind his desk getting ready for the day. I just surprised him, I said, "Coach, Rudy Ruettiger."

He said, "What? What are you doing?"

"I'm at Holy Cross, Coach, but I'm going to come here and get in here and I'm going to play football for you."

He says, "Good. When you get in here, you come and see me."

Right? And I walked out, as I walked out, I said "Man, did I blow that? That's so stupid. Why did you do that, Rudy?" I start crying. I thought, I just blew this whole deal. What an idiot, right?

I saw a group on campus coming across the street, one of the guys said, "Hey Rudy, what are you doing?"

I'm wiping the tears away, man I'm going like this. I said, "I don't know, Coach--"

He said, "Hey, do you need a job?" I don't know why he said that.

He said, "I've got one for ya." One of our camp counselors left. Meet me here in 45 minutes."

ARA PARSEGHIAN
NOTRE DAME HEAD FOOTBALL COACH ('64-'74)

RUDY And I got the job. By being on campus, I got to build more relationships. In fact, they liked me so much they put me on the Notre Dame student government. They never asked me anything about Holy Cross, they assumed I was a Notre Dame student. They said, "Rudy, we never see you in class. What class do you go to?" I pointed to a building, I said, "I go over there." And they would leave it at that.

🎬 CUT TO: RUDY'S BROTHERS TALKING

RUDY'S BROTHER, MICK I got a rejection letter too, from Notre Dame. But he got that same type of letter, but that was his dream.

RUDY'S BROTHER, TIM I think what Rudy's got, he's got that internal switch and he says, "I'm not going to be defeated." And he's had that his entire life.

DENNIS "D-BOB" MCGOWAN I don't know if we lied to each other or encouraged each other by saying, "You're going to make it, you're going to make it, you're gonna make it, you're gonna make it." The difficult, well it's easy, the impossible took a longer time.

RUDY I broke down one day, I said, "Look guys, I'm not a Notre Dame student." In fact, I thought they would get mad, but he said, "We've got to get you in here, man."

DENNIS "D-BOB" MCGOWAN Part of the reason he got in, and I still maintain this, is they got sick of him.

RUDY It's a do or die deal.

🎬 RUDY TALKING TO GROUP

RUDY I opened the letter up at home. Downstairs, where no one could see me. It's a little thicker though. Maybe, if it's a little thicker...

YOUNG MALE Something's good.

RUDY Something's good. When it's thin, man. It's like, shoot. But when it's thick, maybe there's something good in there.

"Oh, my God, I'm in."

So I ran up and showed my dad. He kind of, you made it, you know, type of feeling. You know, because we weren't supposed to go to college.

RUDY'S BROTHER, TIM It was just a great honor,

you know, not only for him, through his perseverance and everything else, but it just goes back to my parents.

RUDY'S BROTHER, MICK But being rejected those other times, from Notre Dame, it sent a sense of pride to all the brothers and the sisters. You know, because, in Joliet, you don't go to Notre Dame.

TERRY GANNON It was validation. It was proving to all those people back in Joliet and elsewhere that doubted him. That, see, he goes after something that nobody else believes is going to happen, and he gets it done.

RUDY'S BROTHER, FRANCIS But then my dad wanted him to still work for the summer, he says, "I can't, I've got to try out for the football team so..."

PAUL BERGAN
RUDY MOVIE FOOTBALL COORDINATOR

IN THE 70S, THE ATMOSPHERE OF NOTRE DAME WAS, YOU KNOW, I GUESS THE BIGGEST THING, IT WAS A LOT LOUDER.

PAUL BERGAN The games were always exciting. I think the thing about the 70s, was there was a different feel for football. It was a different type of football that was being played. And I think the big thing about it is everybody was trying to cut costs, and save money, and cut scholarships and the walk-ons were not encouraged. So I think it was a little different, yeah.

GA. TECH 7   DOWN 3
NOTRE DAME 10   YDS TO GO 9
QUARTER 4   BALL ON 49

OFFICIAL TIME :01

LONGINES

1973 RANKINGS

IRISH FOOTBALL REVIEW

1. NOTRE DAME
2. OHIO STATE

MICHAEL DANCH
ASSOCIATE ATHLETICS DIRECTOR
NOTRE DAME

MICHAEL DANCH In those days, they were in the hunt. Notre Dame had some really great players. Ross Brown was introduced in the college football Hall of Fame or Rory Fry, one of the great players in Notre Dame history in defense. Both guys were like 6'4" and 265. You know, Rudy's 5'9", maybe, and then 190-195lbs.

"ACADEMICALLY, I'M NOT SUPPOSED TO BE AT NOTRE DAME. ATHLETICALLY, I'M NOT SUPPOSED TO BE HERE."

When I got in as a Junior, what's interesting, you get into Notre Dame academically, but now the football deal. And I'm going to have a chance to go to fall workouts.

LARRY MORIARTY
HOUSTON OILERS ('83-'86)
KANSAS CITY CHIEFS ('86-'88)

LARRY MORIARTY Walk-ons are disrespected. And it's sad to see, but it's really... if you take a young kid in high school that's in 10th, 11th, and 12th grade and he's the biggest and best and the fastest and the strongest and he's had his ass kissed his whole life. So, when they come into Notre Dame and they're highly recruited, and every one of them are, then they see the walk-ons. They think they're so much better than the walk-ons, they're not humble.

RUDY Now when you're a walk-on, this is what's fascinating about a walk-on, they don't treat ya very nice. Which means they really don't care, because they've already got their players. When I walked on that football field for the first time, most walk-ons saw the first scrimmage and got scared, because all you see is a cloud of dust. And the kids walk away going, do I want a part in that? Because they hit. Now you've got a choice. Do you really want this? They're not cutting ya, it's your choice if you want to hold that bag and get beat up some more, right? They don't cut walk-ons. You're going to quit or you're going to stick it out.

DENNIS "D-BOB" MCGOWAN I'd go to practice quite a bit when he played. You know, they just beat the hell out of him. In practice, you've got to play against the first team.

PAT SARB
FORMER TEAMMATE

PAT SARB Sometimes the coaches would want you to back off on the prep squad, on the suicide squad.

DENNIS "D-BOB" MCGOWAN But Rudy was a guy that wouldn't back off. And while I'm walking off practice with him, I said, "Rudy, what the hell are you doing this for, man?" He says, "You know, people go to school and play football for four years and never get to play Notre Dame, and I get to play Notre Dame every day." And I go, "Oh, my God, that was really a cool thing to say."

RUDY Naive, but true.

If you get in the game, it's better than just looking. And saying, "Am I that good? I can't run as fast as him." Who cares?

When I walked on, what was the key? Building that relationship with Coach Parseghian. Walking in and out of his office. Remember, I thought it was so stupid, this is nuts. What did I do? It paid off. Because when I walked up, he remembered me.

What's interesting, the coaches again picked out what? Character. The good coaches.

You know what it's like not getting a uniform like the other guys? You know what it's like they put you in the basement locker room and they give you white pants instead of gold pants? And your jock bag is not washed. And ah, you say, "Hey manager, can you wash my bag so I feel like I'm somebody?" My dream was just to get my bag washed and get my gold pants.

RUDY [PRETENDING TO TALK TO TEAM MANAGER] "Hey, can you put my name on your depth chart?" Because your names never on the depths charts. They make up your name, they put it there. Coaches come in and say "Who's this guy?"

RUDY I had some big goals, to me. But they were small to the scholarship players. Who picks up on that? Coaches, they watch you.

They watch how you get hit, how you get up. How you get hit, how you get up. We need this kid. Play more like this kid, with heart.

🎬 LARRY TALKING TO CAMERA

LARRY MORIARTY It's been, what, 37 years and it still seems like yesterday. Walking in there, working out, and with all these big Adonis recruited from all over the country, and walk in and see little Rudy. He was a warrior.

RUDY Contributing, that's what I learned. If I can contribute to the football team at Notre Dame, then I'm somebody.

🎬 IMAGE OF NEWSPAPER HEADLINE

RUDY New coach comes in, a new rule comes in. NCAA, only 60 guys can dress at home. Wait a minute, 60? That means 50 guys are not going to dress. I'm not one of those.

SOUTH BEND, INDIANA, MONDAY, DECEMBER 16, 1974

Ara Resigns as N.D. Coach

DAN DEVINE

🎬 RUDY WALKING AROUND JOYCE CENTER ARENA

RUDY This is my room. Now it's a mail distribution center. This is where I lived. All my buddies when there was a big show would pile into my room. As soon as I opened that door, it was like a Chinese fire drill. They would all pile out and go to the concert.

JOYCE CENTER ARENA
NOTRE DAME

ROSS BROWNER
ND DEFENSIVE END ('73–'77)

ROSS BROWNER Rudy was always around us. He took Willie Fry and myself to his dorm room. His dorm room was not in the stadium, like in the movie, but it was in the ACC, The Joyce Center. And I said, "Boy, how did you get this room?" I said, "I want a room…" Because it had the track and it had the courts and everything, you had the weight facilities. And I was like, "Man, this is great to stay here."

MICHAEL DANCH They had two apartments in the building at the time. One was down at gate eight, where Rudy lived, and one was upstairs, where the Monogram club currently is. For insurance purposes, the building needed to have somebody occupying the building 24 hours a day. So, we had those two apartments, and at the time there was no security that was assigned to our building so we were able to let some people live in the building. Rudy, obviously, needed a place to stay while he was going to school. So, that was his room and board.

RUDY RECALLING A STORY DURING HIS TOUR

RUDY I brought a jersey out to Elvis, and I gave it to a guy and he gave it to Elvis, in the back of the car, and he gave me a hound dog, a rubber hound dog. I gave it to my sister. Years later, about three years ago, I'm speaking, and this guy comes up to me, he says, "I met you in 1975 at Notre Dame." I said, "You did?" I'm supposed to remember that, right?" He says, "No, you probably don't, but you gave a jersey to Elvis." I said, "How would you know that?" He said, "I was in the backseat. I'm his stepbrother." I said, "Oh, my God, what a small world." Isn't that wild?

RUDY CONTINUES THE TOUR

RUDY It was my job to clean up the stadium after games, right? This is where I stood for the games, right here. This is where I sat with my little broom. I would clean up. If there's sweat, I would wipe it up. It was my job, right? I'm on the cover of *Sports Illustrated*. Bill Walton's going up for a rebound and I'm right between his legs. Right here. This is my home.

THIS IS STILL A TRUE STORY

CUT TO: PAT SARB TALKING TO CAMERA

PAT SARB Rudy started showing up, I'd see him on campus, junior year, 1974, Rudy came out and they had a walk-on tryout. And he came out and he was able to make the team as a defensive end. By senior year, of course, all the seniors would love to get a chance to go in and play. Towards the end of the season, I knew Rudy and other walk-ons really wanted to play and the odds were extremely small that they'd even get a chance to be on the dress squad.

PAT SARB
NO CORNERBACK ('73-'75)

DENNIS "D-BOB" MCGOWAN Parseghian promised him that he would have a chance to dress. And, of course, Devine had no obligation to put this kid in. I mean, it was terrible.

PAT SARB The NCAA had restrictions on how many players could dress. It was a cost-saving measure the NCAA was trying to put into place. So, the Thursday night before a home game, the coaches would post the dress squad.

RUDY I'll never forget looking at that final dress list. My name wasn't on it. I got really angry. I said, "All this work for nothing."

RUDY'S BROTHER, FRANCIS A couple days prior I had talked to him, and then his name wasn't on the dress list. He was all upset and everything and he said he's going to quit. I said, "What do you mean you're going to quit?" I said, "You've got one game left, what are you going to quit for?" He said, "Because I'm not dressing," and hung up the phone.

RUDY I'll never forget, I walk around the corner, walking back to my room, and there was the janitor, limping.

I'm calling the coach every name in the

book. Blah, blah, blah, you know. I looked at him, and I said, "Why are you limping, man?"

He says, "I have a prosthesis. I lost my leg to sugar diabetes."

"I see you never complain, man, you never whine."

"No, I love where I'm at. I love coming to work. I love this place."

And that turned me around. What am I feeling sorry for myself for? So, I went back out to practice. Went through the drills, it's a walkthrough. Then Devine, Dan Devine, gives us a talk. Then he gives housekeeping stuff, and he says, "We've got a change in the dress list."

COMMENTATOR Fighting Irish, around their playing field is their co-captains: Jim Stock for the defense, Ed Bauer for the offense go out.

PAT SARB So the Thursday before the Georgia Tech game, my name showed up on the list. Ed Bauer, one of our co-captains, walked up to me in the locker room and said, "Would you be willing to sit out so Rudy could dress?" And I honestly didn't hesitate, and I knew that that was the only chance he would ever have.

RUDY Pat Sarb gave up his uniform, that's a big, big moment. Man, my adrenaline was high.

VOICEOVER Who found out first that he got on the football team?

RUDY'S BROTHER, JOHN I did.

RUDY'S BROTHER, FRANICS No, you, suited up...

RUDY'S BROTHER, JOHN Well, come on Frank. I got the call. He told everybody that he did (pointing to Francis), but I answered the phone first. He said, "Hey, I'm suiting up for the game. Tell Mom and Dad." So, I went up and told my dad. And he said, "Betty, we're leaving for the game."

RUDY'S BROTHER, FRANICS You know how the players huddle up underneath the tunnel? Him and I are in the end zone, we're kind of looking over, looking for the little guy. And all of a sudden they pull him out front. I said, "John Boy, look it, there he is, there he is."

I just started crying. I just started crying when I saw that. It was unbelievable.

COMMENTATOR AND MCLAUGHLIN HAS THE BALL TEED UP, PUTS HIS HAND IN THE AIR, GETS THE SIGNAL FROM THE OFFICIAL. AND NOTRE DAME IS GONNA GET IT UNDER WAY.

RUDY BUT YOU KNOW WHAT NOW KICKS IN, I WANT TO PLAY.

COMMENTATOR NOTRE DAME IS OUT OF THE HUDDLE. IT IS 3RD DOWN AND FIVE. SLAGER PITCH'S IT BACK JUST AS HE'S HIT, HEAVENS HAS THE BALL AND HEAVENS GOES IN FOR A TOUCHDOWN.

RUDY WE SCORED, WE GET A FIELD GOAL, WE SCORE, WE GET ANOTHER SCORE.

COMMENTATOR JEROME HEAVENS, HERE IS THE EXTRA POINT, HIGH INTO THE STANDS, IT'S GOOD.

GEORGIA TECH vs. NOTRE DAME

RUDY IN ORDER FOR ME TO PLAY, WE HAVE TO SCORE SO WE CAN GO ON DEFENSE. IT'S NOT GOING TO HAPPEN, THERE'S ONLY A MINUTE LEFT IN THE GAME.

COMMENTATOR 38 SECONDS TO GO IN THE GAME. NOTRE DAME 3RD IN GOAL OF THE THREE-YARD LINE OF GEORGIA TECH.

ROSS BROWNER COACH SAID, "NO, NO, NO, NO, NO, WE'LL JUST RUN THE CLOCK OUT." AND THE GUYS ON OFFENSE DECIDED, WE GOT IN A HUDDLE AND SAID, "WE'RE GOING TO SCORE."

RUDY BY A MIRACLE, WE SCORED.

COMMENTATOR ALLOCCO ROLLS OUT, PITCH'S HIS BACK WHERE THE BALL IS, THEY'RE NOT, TOUCHDOWN, NOTRE DAME.

ANNOUNCER WITH THE SCORE, NOTRE DAME 24, GEORGIA TECH 3.

COMMENTATOR JEROME HEAVENS, HERE IS THE EXTRA POINT, HIGH INTO THE STANDS, IT'S GOOD.

RUDY NOW I'M ON DEFENSE, NOW THE STUDENT BODY STARTS CHANTING, "RUDY." SOME OF THE KIDS SAID, "PUT HIM IN THE GAME. PUT THE KID IN THE GAME."

RUDY'S BROTHER, FRANICS WHEN THEY START CHANTING HIS NAME AT THE GAME, THESE PEOPLE SAID, "WHO'S RUDY?" WE STOOD UP, WE KIND OF JUST STOOD UP, HIM AND I AT THE SAME TIME, AND SAID, "THAT'S OUR BROTHER."

RUDY THEY JUST THREW ME IN ON THE KICKOFF.

COMMENTATOR PAT MCLAUGHLIN WILL KICKOFF WITH 28 SECONDS TO GO. LINE DRIVE THE BALL INTO AND OUT OF THE END ZONE.

RUDY I DIDN'T KNOW WHERE TO GO AFTER THAT. I'M RUNNING OFF THE FIELD, "WHERE DO I GO?"

ROSS BROWNER HE WAS SO EXCITED, YOU KNOW, WE JUST SAID, "RUN OUT ON THE FIELD." AND I SAID, "RUDY, YOU'RE IN FOR ME. I SAID GO IN AT LEFT END, GO STRAIGHT, GO NOW. THEY'RE GETTING READY TO BREAK OUT THE HUDDLE."

COMMENTATOR GEORGIA TECH WILL PUT THE BALL IN OFFENSE, FIRST AND 10, 20 YARD LINE. RUDY ALLEN, WITH 28 SECONDS TO GO DROPS TO THROW FOR GEORGIA TECH.

RUDY RUDY ALLEN LEANS BACK HIS FIRST PASS, HE MISSES AND THERE'S FIVE SECONDS LEFT IN THE GAME. I'LL NEVER FORGET LOOKING UP AT THE CLOCK.

WE LINED UP ACTUALLY RIGHT HERE. I'M DIGGING IN LIKE THIS.

COMMENTATOR WELL GEORGIA TECH FELL BEHIND AND UNABLE TO PASS, THEY'VE JUST BEEN UNABLE TO GET BACK IN THIS GAME.

RUDY AND THE BALL SNAPPED, I GO TO THE LEFT AND I JUKED TO THE RIGHT AND THERE WAS RUDY ALLEN.

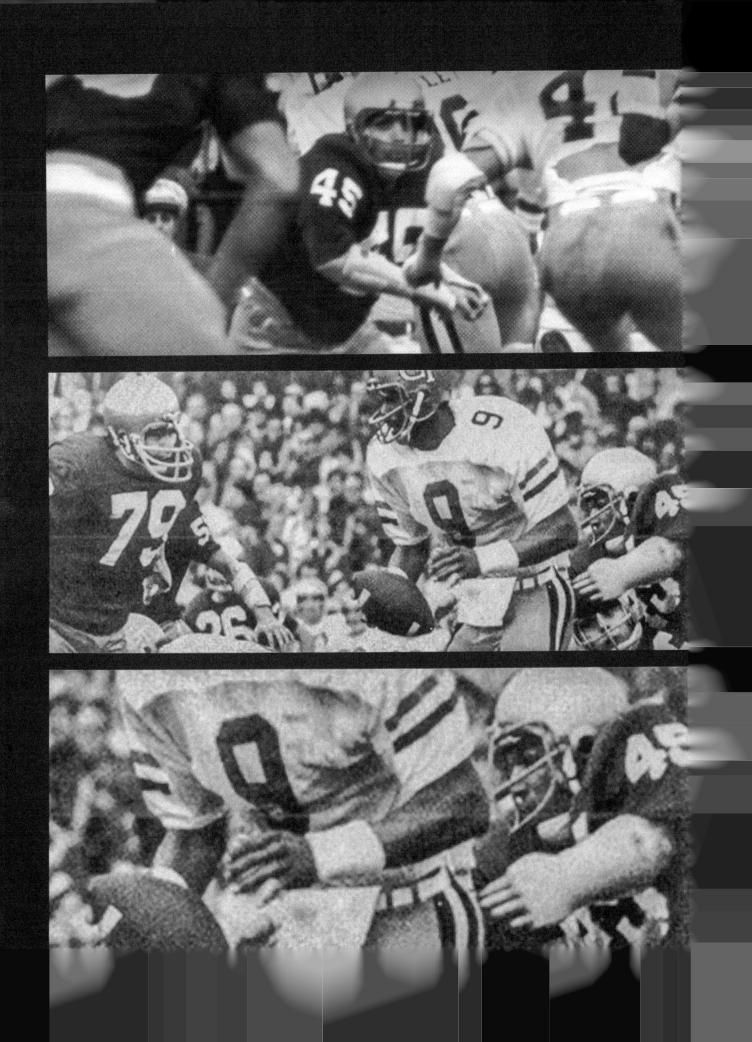

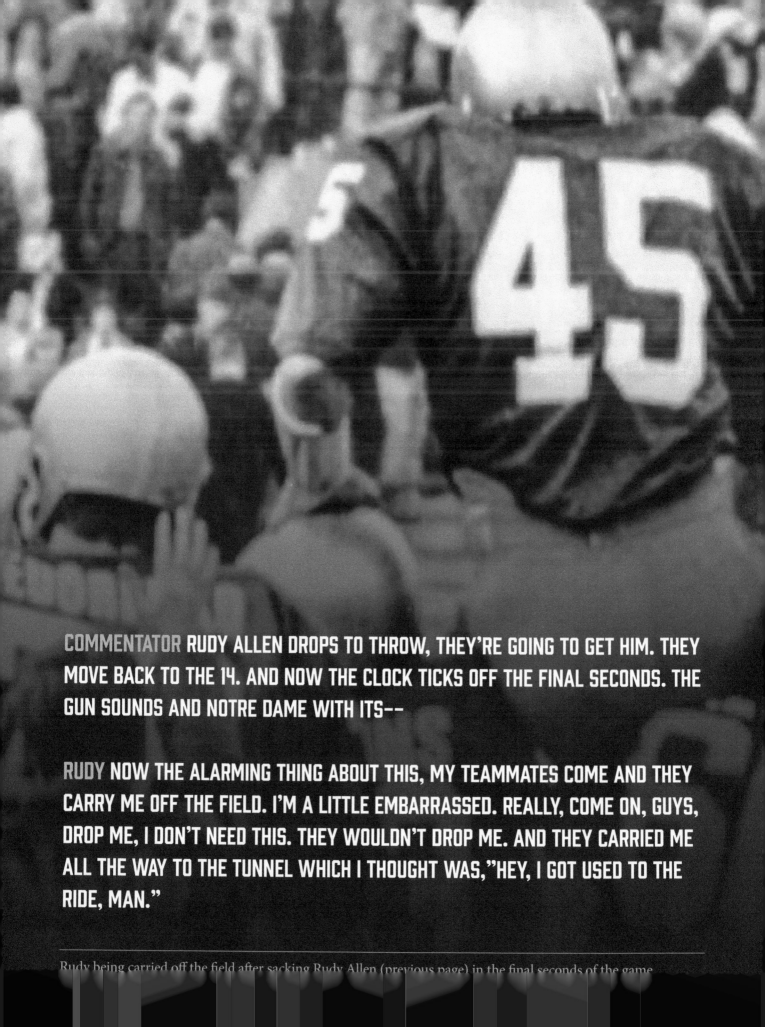

COMMENTATOR RUDY ALLEN DROPS TO THROW, THEY'RE GOING TO GET HIM. THEY MOVE BACK TO THE 14. AND NOW THE CLOCK TICKS OFF THE FINAL SECONDS. THE GUN SOUNDS AND NOTRE DAME WITH ITS--

RUDY NOW THE ALARMING THING ABOUT THIS, MY TEAMMATES COME AND THEY CARRY ME OFF THE FIELD. I'M A LITTLE EMBARRASSED. REALLY, COME ON, GUYS, DROP ME, I DON'T NEED THIS. THEY WOULDN'T DROP ME. AND THEY CARRIED ME ALL THE WAY TO THE TUNNEL WHICH I THOUGHT WAS,"HEY, I GOT USED TO THE RIDE, MAN."

Rudy being carried off the field after sacking Rudy Allen (previous page) in the final seconds of the game.

JEFF ROSS
FILM PRODUCER

JEFF ROSS Everybody says, here's a guy who wanted to play football at Notre Dame, went through all the disappointments and the struggles and the adversity and he finally obtained his dream. And they think, "Gee that's great." And it is. But what defines Rudy is that that didn't stop him. The thing with Rudy, and it should be with all of us, is that:

ONCE YOU OBTAIN THAT GOAL, WHATEVER IT IS, THERE'S A NEW GOAL.

RUDY I'll never forget walking in the locker room, Coach had me say something.

"Rudy, you got something to say?" Because everybody's excited.

I said, "I've been waiting for this. For my whole life, I've been waiting for this." That's all I said and went back to taking my jersey off.

I'll never forget, this sports writer comes up to me. Good sports writer, he said, "Kid!" He said, "Rudy, right?"

I said, "yeah."

"They were cheering your name, no one knew you. I didn't know ya. They didn't even know who they were cheering for. You don't even have a name on your jersey. What's the story, that story about?"

I didn't have time to tell him.

He said, "Heck, this stuff I just witnessed out here only happens in Hollywood."

He just planted a seed, that's all he did. And that was it.

🎬 CUT TO: RUDY ON USC CAMPUS, LOS ANGELES

MAN You see the names on the top?

RUDY I know, Stephen Spielberg Building. Is that awesome? And George Lucas, look at that.

🎬 RUDY ADDRESSING STUDENTS AT USC

RUDY Work on yourself, that's the key. Believe in you and it all happens. Believe. I'm telling ya, that's the key. It took me 10 years to get *Rudy* made. I came out to Hollywood with just a story. Not knowing anything about Hollywood. Would you all agree inspiration is the key to your success?

MALE Yes.

RUDY You can know whatever you want to know, but it doesn't do you any good until, you what, you get inspired. Now it's important for you to watch movies, all movies. Because why? It's your career and you learn. I watch inspirational movies. *Rocky, Hoosiers, Field of Dreams.* All of a sudden I've got a movie idea. I didn't graduate from Notre Dame and say I'm gonna do a movie until that sports writer in the locker room said this only happens in Hollywood.

TERRY GANNON The thing about Rudy is, even after that game, he didn't become larger than life. He had to go make a living. Whether it was selling cars or Amway and a number of different things. Early on, Rudy told me that he had an idea that he's going to make a movie about his life. And I thought, "Oh, that's great, good. Good luck with that." No chance.

RUDY'S BROTHER, FRANCIS Who goes to Notre Dame and says I'm going to make a movie, we want to use your campus? You know, he just played the one game. You know, just stuff doesn't happen like that.

LARRY MORIARTY Rudy had an apartment, a condominium across the street from the campus. He had ex-players and celebrities and coaches at his house, so you always wanted to get out of your dorm room and go over to the house and hang around with Rudy. It was easy to believe that his dream was going to come true, and that he was going to put this movie together.

PAUL BERGAN Every Thursday, the boys and I, we'd come down and sit on his porch or in his house and we'd just talk and kind of dream. And Rudy had this dream about the movie. And he kept talking about it and talking about it.

THE BERGAN BOYS
RUDY MOVIE FOOTBALL COORDINATORS

THE BERGAN BOYS In these chalk talk sessions we would hear kind of updates on his process and what he was going through and how committed he was, but the fact is it didn't look like it was going to ever materialize to come to the movie that it came to be.

RUDY ADDRESSING STUDENTS AT USC

RUDY Notre Dame, basically, I thought Notre Dame would get onboard right away, they basically said no. We don't want anything to do with Hollywood.

DENNIS "D-BOB" MCGOWAN And Rudy went to the head Priest and the Priest said, "We do not want another football movie here." The first one was done in 1941 with Ronald Reagan, *Knute Rockne All American*.

RUDY TALKING TO CAMERA

RUDY Notre Dame got kind of sick and tired of me showing up on campus. They already had their image: Knute Rockne. I've got to sell Notre Dame on a new face.

DENNIS "D-BOB" MCGOWAN For Rudy, he came up with the right answer. He says, "This is not a Notre Dame football movie, Father. This is a Notre Dame love story."

RUDY It was a message, I wanted to deliver a message of hope, through my journey, because that's what it was.

RUDY ADDRESSING STUDENTS AT USC

RUDY They made me sign a letter saying, do not walk into this campus again ever talking about a movie.

🎬 RUDY CONTINUES, AT REUNION PARTY

RUDY Because we had a little meeting, and the meeting lasted about a minute, and they said, that was it, I had to sign off on it. I didn't abandon the deal, I just put it on pause.

🎬 RUDY TALKING TO CAMERA

RUDY At Notre Dame, they didn't get it. In Hollywood, one guy got it. It was a mailman.

🎬 RUDY CONTINUES STORY IN VARIOUS LOCATIONS

RUDY Okay, that's the hotel we had our final meeting and what happened was, a hotel manager sees me and he asked how the meeting went.

I said, "John, it didn't go too good."

He said, "Hey, my brother's coming to town. He wants to talk to ya."

I said, "Really, about what?"

"I don't know, I keep telling him your story, I keep telling him what you're doing. He's interested in talking to ya."

I said, "all right."

"Will you go to Barnaby's and have a pizza with him?"

We're sitting in a booth like we are now. Ordered a pizza. He said, "Now tell me your story." And I told him the story.

And he looks right at me. He said, "That's a movie." I said, "How would you know that's a movie?"

"Because we put *Hoosiers* together. It's a movie. I think you should tell Angelo that." Angelo Pizzo who wrote *Hoosiers*. "Will you fly out and meet Angelo if I set-up a meeting?"

I said, "Absolutely." I contacted my friend Alan Mintz to help me get out to Santa Monica, because he's from California.

ALAN MINTZ
ASSOCIATE PRODUCER OF RUDY

ALAN MINTZ So I pick him up and I ask where we're going. He gives me the address and it's a restaurant on the west side. So we go to the restaurant and we sit there for two hours. Angelo doesn't show up. And I said, "Well that's that." And he says, "No, we're going to find him."

RUDY And I walked outside, I see a mailman, smiling and happy. You don't see many mailmen happy.

🎬 RUDY ADDRESSING STUDENTS AT USC

And I looked right at him. I said, "Thank you, man, I needed that smile." You know what he said, "Where are you from?"

I said, "Indiana."

He said, "What are you out here for?"

"Oh, I'm trying to pitch an idea for a movie. And the guy didn't show up yet."

He said, "Really, what's your story?" And I tell him. He got passionate.

"So what's that guy's name again?"

I said, "Angelo Pizzo."

"I know where he lives. I deliver his mail."

He said, "You follow me. What I'm about to do, I'm not supposed to do. But I love your story. That's my story."

I followed him. I'm going to myself, is this right? Should I do this? This is wrong.

ALAN MINTZ So he knocks on the door. Angelo answers the door, half asleep. These writers are up all night writing. And he said, "Who are you?"

He said, "I'm Rudy and we had a meeting."

I can't remember exactly what Angelo said, but it was probably not printable.

RUDY He said immediately, he apologized. He was up all night rewriting a script.

▸ RUDY PAUSING HIS STORY TO DIRECTLY ADDRESS THE STUDENTS OF USC.

Now, I want you to listen to what I'm about to say to you. Sometimes you've got to do things you don't like to do. Sometimes you ignore the things you're best at because you don't think you're good at what you do. You want to do different things, but you know God's given you a talent and the skill to do what you do. Now stick with it.

ALAN MINTZ He said, "I had a great success with *Hoosiers*." He said, "I don't want to be pigeonholed as a writer of Indiana sports stories."

RUDY Then he says, "Besides, I hate Notre Dame." He gave me two goofy thoughts, but he gave me a good thought: You got a good story. That's when I hung on. I said, let's go to lunch. He said, "I don't want to

talk about a movie." I said, "No, no, I'm not." I learned to build a relationship with him for two more years. I said, he will write *Rudy*. He didn't know that yet.

▸ RUDY WITH HIS BROTHERS

RUDY Hey, what was your reaction to, I'm always, I never asked you, what did you think when the movie was actually greenlighted?

RUDY'S BROTHER, FRANCIS Well, I thought, I said, wow, it's gonna happen.

RUDY Hold on here, I gotta tell you this story, Paul, you'll love this. We come to Squeaky's house, and we needed some money to get this thing going. Go to Squeaky's, "Hey Squeaky..." I never saw an exit so fast. Soon as the wife says, "Get him out of here."

RUDY'S BROTHER, TIM He comes, he says, "You're gonna invest in my movie." Grace said, "We ain't got really a whole lot of money in out pot right now, we're just starting out."

RUDY'S BROTHER, MICK He was persistent. People call him a pest at times, but I see him as persistent to a point of, this story needs to be told.

🎬 RUDY ADDRESSING STUDENTS AT USC

RUDY Right before I flew out here, my boss called me into his office and fired me because he got sick and tired of me going out to California.

🎬 RUDY TALKING ON CAMERA

RUDY I went back to work as a grass cutter. I didn't want a real job anymore, I just wanted a job to put food on my table, pay my mortgage.

One day, I walked into my condo, there was a little red light on the answering machine blinking, just blinking. And I answered it, put it on rewind, it said, "Rudy, Angelo, call me." Holy cow, he sounded matter of fact like he always is.

I called and he says, "Well, your movie was greenlighted."

I said, "What?"

"Your movie's done, they commissioned me to write it."

I said, "What are you talking about?"

🎬 RUDY SHOWING THE SCRIPT FOR THE MOVIE

Here's the first script Angelo ever gave me,

right there. It's hard to read a script if you don't know how to read it, but I read it like a book and it just, it was good. I said, "Angelo, that was good." He said, "Did you understand it?" I said, "Some of it."

So I started making notes.

Thank god for a guy who applied to Notre Dame, got turned down, and ended up at Michigan State, and was a walk on at Michigan State. He's the president of Columbia Pictures who had the right and the look and the money and the say-so to make movies happen. He called the guys in from *Hoosiers* because he loved that movie. He wants another sports movie.

I never told Angelo what Notre Dame's attitude was, there was no need to. They never asked, they just assumed Notre Dame was gonna be for this project. So Angelo does all the research, six months later, he comes back with the script. Now we gotta go get Notre Dame in line because we're gonna start production here in two months and we gotta let them know what's happening.

I said, "Dude, we can't do that."

He said, "What do you mean?"

"Because Notre Dame made me sign a letter, I can't come and talk about this movie anymore, they're gonna bar me from campus."

He said, "You're kidding." He said, "They won't do this movie unless Notre Dame's on board, Rudy. Why didn't you tell us this?"

I said, "I know, but I didn't want to tell you the negative, you would have never written the script."

He said, "Oh my god."

The executive producer calls me and says, "Rudy, you got 48 hours to get this movie approved or we're gonna dump it."

MOMENT TO REMEMBER: Extras for the motion picture "Rudy"

'Rudy' 1st movie shot
at ND since 'Rockne'

RUDY David Anspaugh on the way to the meeting, and Angelo, they're nervous, very nervous. "How are we gonna do this?" I said, "Just be yourself." Basically they're gonna check you out real good, see if you got Notre Dame's back, I guess. So they go, and they were in there for like 20 minutes, I don't know what they said, how they said it, they come out with a book in their hand. Father Beauchamp goes like, and I'm not, I'm going, "Oh boy. Did we get it or not?" Because you want to know and they're not saying anything, they're kind of playing stone-faced. Father Beauchamp turns a book, says, "David, this would look good on camera." I said, "Oh my god, this is for real." Done.

Dream merchant

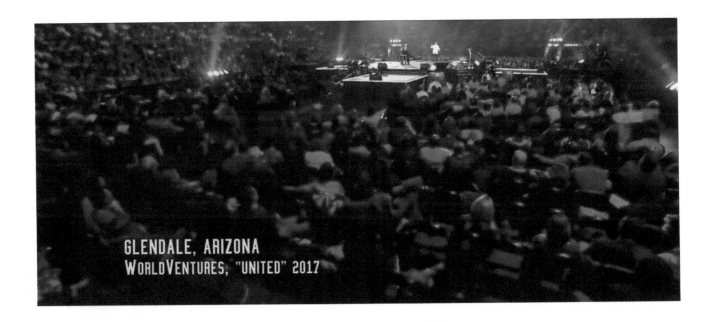

GLENDALE, ARIZONA
WORLDVENTURES, "UNITED" 2017

RUDY Here's the real kicker, this is my last little story to end my speech. We heard a girl on set from Washington, DC, her mother was a senator. She was a great servant leader, remember that word, servant leader. She was so good on set, everybody wanted to have her take care of them because she did everything. Movie wraps, she goes back to Washington, DC. She meets a guy, happened to be the First Lady's brother. They get engaged, they're at dinner with the President, First Lady of the United States, now think about this. The president asks Nicole, "What have you been doing?"

She said, "I've been working on this underdog movie. This movie about this kid who would say, you can never go to Notre Dame, never play, never... And did."

He says, "Underdog? I want to see that movie. Let's bring Rudy to the White House, let's have a movie night in the White House two weeks from Friday, call Rudy..."

And he got excited, she got excited.

I'm in South Bend, Indiana, Nicole calls, "Go to the White House."

I'm walking in the White House, there was the president to greet me, but I look right past him because I did a rewind back to fifth grade, fifth grade, because all the presidential pictures were hanging up on the wall. I went to the fifth

one and I looked up there and said, "Man, that's James Monroe."

DENNIS "D-BOB" MCGOWAN There's a saying by the Catholic order of Christopher's, if everyone lit just one little candle, what a bright world this would be. Well, I think this movie created a pretty big torch. Most of us are "Rudys," you know, you can't relate to Tiger Woods or Michael Jordan, or Joe Namath, or Joe Montana.

YOU KNOW, MOST OF US ARE "RUDYS." WE DON'T KNOW IF WE'RE GONNA BE GREAT, BUT WE'RE GONNA BE BETTER.

To all the children and the kids that feel inferior, believe me, they have a friend in Rudy. That movie was made for you. Thank you.

D-BOB'S GRANDSONS

🎬 RUDY AND D-BOB'S GRANDSONS AT THE CEMETERY

RUDY It's been a while, it was in the snow last time, remember? Yeah, there you go. It was snow, man. You guys were young. There, John Driscoll, right here. Look at that, 1958 - 2002. Now, when were you guys born?

D-BOB'S GRANDSONS 2001.

RUDY 2001, wow. Now, you play lacrosse.

D-BOB'S GRANDSON No.

D-BOB'S GRANDSON Nah, that's me.

RUDY That's you, yeah. And you're a track guy.

D-BOB'S GRANDSON Mmhmm, track, basketball, and football.

RUDY And you're supposed to be at practice right now.

D-BOB'S GRANDSON Yeah. This will be a pretty good excuse to tell my coach, I think it will be fine.

RUDY And Johnny.

D-BOB'S GRANDSON, JOHNNY Football and basketball.

RUDY And basketball. And now here we are years later, as you've grown. My god, it's awesome. You get to meet your dad, but honestly, meeting him this way is still good, because we know he's in a good place. He's in a happy place. And if you want to say a little prayer, we can do that right now. What do you all say? I want you to lead it, my man.

D-BOB'S GRANDSON All right.

ALL Our father...

WHO ART IN HEAVEN, HALLOWED BE THY NAME, THY KINGDOM COME, THY WILL BE DONE, ON EARTH AS IT IS IN HEAVEN, GIVE US THIS DAY OUR DAILY BREAD, FORGIVE US OUR TRESPASSES, AS WE'VE...

THOMAS LOWREY
9TH GRADE

THOMAS LOWREY I just recently turned 14 years old, like a couple weeks ago. I've been drumming all my life, it's my passion, it's my favorite thing to do. I started formal lessons when I was six years old with Rob Ferrell Drum Studio. And I've just been working towards it and working towards it, and it's just, it's what I want to do, there's nothing else I want to do. There's a lot of people who, like, start something, then they give up if they don't like it, you know. I'm not sure, but you know, I've always just stuck with it and kept driving.

PEOPLE LIKE RUDY, THEY'RE THE PEOPLE THAT INSPIRE ME.

And they're the people that want you to keep going and make you feel like you can keep going. It doesn't matter if you're not fit for the job. If you work towards it, anything can happen, anything's possible. If you don't have a Rudy in your life, you need to get one.

IF YOU DON'T HAVE A RUDY IN YOUR LIFE, YOU NEED TO GET ONE.

—THOMAS LOWREY